Praise for AC Benus
from the members of gayauthors.org

Witty, fast-moving, filled with a collection of colourful, eccentric, and somewhat questionable characters. Superbly written and thoroughly entertaining.

—Dodger

Can I just say [Mojo] is akin to *Much Ado About Nothing* or some such Shakespeare play where everyone is double-crossing everyone, and there's so much sex and intrigue and comedy throughout that you don't know whether to gasp or groan or laugh as you read? Each sentence is purposeful and moves the story forward. Your characters sizzle with personalities

—MacGreg

I do not know how to say this – every line AC writes sizzles with innuendo and hidden meaning. Each chapter is golden.

—Will Hawkins

Iced-tea glass raised, I want to toast AC for his untiring efforts – or maybe persistent efforts despite fatigue – to entertain and engage us in every scene.

—knotme

This story is great! I couldn't stop reading. The main characters are very vivid and lovable for all their faults

—Lyssa

Oh, my . . . this writing is incredible . . . it sweeps me away and I am in that place and with those characters. Each chapter is no different: 1,000 words or 10,000, it's never enough.

—Mikiesboy

It's so fun to read an actually witty story with brains behind it; it perks up my evenings.

—Puppilull

Praise for AC Benus
from the members of gayauthors.org

"You positively insist your readers read between the lines." That is how I often feel as a reader of your work, AC. But is it stimulating rather than daunting, and very, very rewarding!
—J. Hunter Dunn

This has been an absolutely marvelous tale from beginning to end. You did it perfectly . . . *Bravissimo, maestro.*
—Parker Owens

What an interesting bunch AC has introduced us to. They are, by turns, over-sexed, under-sexed, scared, and funny. It's like that old movie *It's a Mad, Mad, Mad, Mad World* trying to keep up with who's doing what to whom!
—Mollyhousemouse

Two bananas, a hard-boiled egg, Eleanor Roosevelt, two Gay sailors, a Second World War Luger and some hot spanking. How's that for a writing prompt! This is turning into a masterpiece. No one can ever accuse AC of being predictable.
—Dodger

This is a wonderful book . . . Irreverent, naughty, brilliant, hysterical, and downright entertaining. Thanks a million times for writing it.
—Mikiesboy

You cannot help but be drawn into this wonderfully written story. The characters are vivid and come alive within AC's beautifully described locations. You can see it all in the words he chooses to paint with . . . . First class writing and entertainment
—MichaelS36

Be still, my heart! What a chase scene! What a confrontation . . . Just how many scenes can be sent up? This was like watching a firework show, one spectacular burst after another . . . I was breathless by the end. But I still wanted more.
—Parker Owens

Poetry Available from AC Benus

Hymenaios, or The Marriage of the God of Marriage
A Classical style myth in 2,600 lines of Blank Verse
ebook: ISBN 9781953389091; paperback: ISBN 9781953389084

Summer 2020 – Hell in a Handbasket
A contender for the Pulitzer Prize in poetry, 2021, this collection grapples with the year of pandemic, racial injustice and environmental crisis
ebook: ISBN 9781953389015; paperback: ISBN 9781953389008

The Thousandth Regiment
A Translation of and Commentary on Hans Ehrenbaum-Degele's First World War Poems "Das tausendste Regiment"
ebook: ISBN 1657220583; paperback: ISBN 9781657220584

A Man in a Room, and other poems
Verse following the year when the poet was 21 years old
ebook: ISBN 97817345103; paperback: ISBN 978173456107

The Easiest Thing in the World, and other poems
Marking the third anniversary of the Pulse Nightclub terror attack
ebook: ISBN 9781734561029; paperback: ISBN 9781734561036

Rima Fragmenta, or Fragments of a Rift
Fifty Sonnet for Kevin
ebook: ISBN 9781734561005; paperback: ISBN 9781734561012

First Love: Poems for Ross
For everyone's first love; both bitter and sweet
ebook: ISBN 9781734561081; paperback: ISBN 9781734561098

Poetry Available from AC Benus

Demon Dream
Redemption and shared humanity shine in this retelling of a medieval Japanese legend
ebook: ISBN 9781953389138; paperback: ISBN 9781953389145

Audre Lorde Knows What I Mean – 2021 in Review
A follow-up to Summer 2020, *this collection grapples with the year of the Gop-led Capitol insurrection, racial injustice and the death throes of the environment*
ebook: ISBN 9781953389015; paperback: ISBN 9781953389008

Mikhail Kraminsky, and other poems
Two collections of early poems exploring the pain of youth and being closeted
ebook: ISBN 9781953389152; paperback: ISBN 9781953389169

One Hundred and Fifty-Five Sonnets for Tony
A bold testament to love
ebook: ISBN 9781953389114; paperback: ISBN 9781953389107; hardback: ISBN 9781953389121

Love Looked at Me and Laughed – Poems for Brian
Love is not always easy. Poems to/for/about my first boyfriend
ebook: ISBN 9781953389237; paperback: ISBN 9781953389220
hardback: ISBN 978-1-953389-24-4

Love is Love (Contributor)
Poetry Anthology: In aid of Orlando's Pulse victims and survivors, Lily G. Blunt, Editor, 2016
ebook: ISBN 153514369X; paperback: ISBN 153514369X

»»AC Benus«««

After Days of Rain
and other poems

*from my
twenty-third
year*

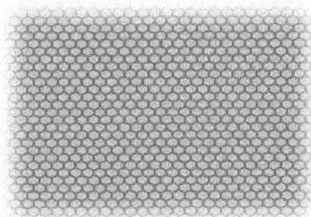

an AC Benus Impression
San Francisco

Grateful acknowledgement is here offered
for the support and encouragement
I've received on the literary site
www.gayauthors.org.

ISBN 978-1-953389-38-1 (ebook)

ISBN 978-1-953389-37-4 (paperback)

AFTER DAYS OF RAIN AND OTHER POEMS:

FROM MY TWENTY-THIRD YEAR.

Cover photo:
Unsplash.com – Adrian Swancar

Library of Congress Control Number: 2023909145

Contents

Part I:
After Days of Rain
various poems

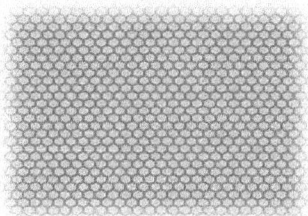

Poem No. 1 [1]

. . . The Stench of Words . . .

The future stretches ahead of me
    in vast array
speaking of the wonder of a million things
    there are yet to say

Poem No. 2

Which is the real America,
in which section can it be found?

Which song is her native sound?

Which is the land of Liberty,
which color are her native sons?

Are they the victims or cause?
Rich face, poor face, in bus, in beemer?
Think them victim; feel them the cause

Poem No. 3 [2]

The war began on the evening news
    5:30 in the center of the country
    and Baghdad burns.

Mitchell of the Senate could not be found –
    in Brooks Brothers it seems he was
    looking at new shirts
    and Baghdad burns.

Dinner all across the land
    a time to relax and watch TV
    but the world came home suddenly –
    Dan Rather had a lump in his throat
    and Baghdad burns.

Poem No. 4

Lyric Sonnet:

Where is the real America?
In which section can it be found?
There, in mass-made suburbia,
Which is proud to lack the profound.
What color are Her native sons?
Be they the victims; be they the cause;
Rich face; poor face – need they the guns?
Crime be the reason; death be the cause?
Which is the Land of Liberty?
Are you free to live on the street,
To cut your taxes through charity,
Destroy all opposition you meet?

    Yes and no; the answer alarms
      they who think about it.
    This land where no one group harms
      the rights of all those born to it?

Poem No. 5

It flows
through the hills
to the sea

It sweeps
nearby me
endlessly

It knows
what to find
inside of me

It creeps
and I can see
endlessly.

Poem No. 6

Prelude:

Optimism wanes, reality finds
I am alone
Help distains, sorrow binds
I am alone
Memories pain, worry reminds
I am alone.

Poem:

Boy on the train
give me your love before your name
tell me if you know how I feel
Let me know if it is the same
that look which I pray can be real

An idiot I must be
a romantic drowning rat
to pin myself to his soul
An idiot I must be
what use has he for me
a romantic drowning rat
who wants to be in love.

Boy on the train
please look at me again that way
Let me find the courage to reply
fortify me with words to say
please look at me that way

That look for the half-second it lives
free from giver to my passing eyes
shouts its accusation, flaunts its invitation
and tries to comfort the fact it knows;
I look away because first it accuses
what I want no one to know
that I want no one to see me reply.

That look which I pray can be real
Let me know if it is the same
tell me if you know how I feel
give me your love before your name
Boy on the train.

Poem No. 7

俳句：

悲哀勝つ万事
日常の顔
朝電車で

[Haiku:

Hiai katsu banji
nichijoh no kao
asa densha de]

[Sorrow pervades all;
routine faces, routine lives
on the morning train

Sorrow wins it all
on the everyday faces
of the morning train

Total mis'ry plays
o'er the accustomed faces
'pon the morning's train]

Poem No. 8

Prelude:

The morning asks me
of my restless sleep
why do I want to need.

I want not a thing
every need taken care of
except the need to be wanted

Will the evening find me
in this same old sleep
asking why do I want to be needed

Will the morning find me
where it left me before
too old to be lonely
too young not to try.

Poem:

I don't want to be
twenty-three
too much of the world
I failed to see
through the eyes
of twenty-two
and it scares me
to be twenty-three.

Postlude:

Lovely lonely presence,
lifted from my heart.

I don't want to be
twenty-three.
Too much of the world
I failed to see
through the eyes
of twenty-two
and it scare me
to see twenty-three.

Lovely lonely presence,
lifted from my heart,
faces the frightening pretense
as there from the start.
Say goodbye to my love.
All of it was yours.
for time immortal,
I offered my love

Bid farewell to my love.
It no more rests on yours.
Resignation's portal,
you wanted from the start

Lovely lonely presence,
lifted from my heart.

Seeming; seeming freedom,
clamped onto my mind,
no longer feels them,
as something left behind.

Poem No. 9

Step back,
Take the perspective of the fates:
In fact, take it from them.
After all, it is yours.

Poem No. 10

In the air
all the past, future and probables
are in the air

I don't like to be
twenty-three
the only thing it means
is there were twenty-three years
I failed to see

Twenty-three years
I failed to be
the anniversary
for what it means
of what I failed to be

and so I am in the air
all the past, future, and probables
keep me there, in the air.

Poem No. 11

The world wakes
and yawns it colors
anew.

From its frigid slumber
a miracle becomes its dream
that everything can be as it
was before.

Finding its will
to live and give
anew.

    <u>Spring Song</u>

Poem No. 12

    Prelude:

There's a place I pass,
   where hope has a price

Mystery swarms with its silent patrons
   who for fear of ill-luck, make not a noise

No one would dare shout a word
   in this holy shrine of the might-be

I walk more softly as I began to approach
   this silent place where hope has a price

I think why play the lottery,
   but such serious faces tell me otherwise.

They say it is a chance to live
   the chance to make life what it should be

Mystery swarms with its silent patrons
   who for fear of ill-luck make not a sound

Time is running away from this place,
   too soon they'll be too old to live

That is their worst fear,
   the one that brings them back

To the place I pass
   where hope has a price.

   Poem:

Perhaps in my sleep, I can chance to dream
that I am as great as death itself.

In my slumber, I can make myself anew
a Don Juan of love and all life.

There can I be safe, mater of it all
No dues or debts to pay or lend.

In my dreams can I find what I am not
there in my sleep, away from life, can I live.

There in the world of my self-liberty
can I be as great as death its very self.

For Death is the true measure of all
the counterbalance on the scale of meaning
only in my dreams can I be its equal.

    Postlude:

In the land of the gray-haired youth,
    I have a chance to spy myself.
Amongst these people of smoke,
    I can see the smoke of my heart.
I can see the gray of my youth,
    I can find the same beginnings.

    If life is only the chance to live,
    then it is chance I've yet to take.
    Silently I step to the window,
    and pay my price for hope.
    And play my chance to live.
    And prey I'm not too old.

Poem No. 13

The progress of the Heart
can be one the Mind envies,
but never is it so in reverse.

Poem No. 14

With every day, with every Line,
new adventure can be seen.
For those who look, they will find –
Tales of the heart, the hapless, the obscene

That look, for the half-second it lives,
free from giver, to my passing eyes,
shouts its accusation, flaunts it incantation
and tries to comfort, the fact it knows.
I look away because first it accuses
what I want no one to know.
That I want no one to see me reply.

Poem No. 15

Regrets are the easiest thing in the world to avoid,
and the hardest to live with.

Poem No. 16

Deep in the settled night,
They lean against the wall
Waiting for the person right
For whom to make their call.
They needn't say a word,
For eyes can hold a tongue
From making words absurd,
From getting the action done.
These boys of the station,
Looking for nightly work,
By the walls of every nation
Eyes look for their evening work

Poem No. 17

Why is loneliness so lovely;
    what endearment can it offer.
To be young and lonely;
    beauty suggests mutual suffering.

Poem No. 18

How to say in words, what Webster never found;
Is there no help from all the lives that have been?
A whisper from the past, or only a sound;
I look for their words this poem to begin.

Poem No. 19

The night finds itself mature
when its bicycle Romeos
find their rentable Juliets

A seat too small for one
becomes quite cozy for two –
anticipation makes it so –
as they ride home to the night
though two different ambitions it finds

Boys with two wheels
and girls with short skirts
need only one seat
for they have only one night

Rentable love
no one pretends it is such
only fools on the sidelines
can look and still be that blind,
to make pretentions of so little,
after all, they know it's only
rentable love

Poem No. 20

Prelude:

When the bicycle Romeos
Find their mini-skirted loves;
When the windows fling open
So sleeping men may find
The solitude of a drunken room

When the taximen refuse
The stumbling hands of those
Who from pit and penthouse
Now glide onto the street
In search of elusive home

When the last trains make it in
And the lonely riders,
Who rode for the finding,
May take their pick of those
Gentlemen waiting to be found

The price for the evening, I'm not sure what it is
One heart for the borrowing, to give one night of relief
A pint of new whiskey, to make numb a few hours
While the fact of seeking, empowers they to be found.

The evening grows old
And gives up a sigh
When the two wheeled Romeos
Rent their short-skirted prize;
When all for sale, is sold.

Poem:

Then the evening reclined
Into the arms of the night –
Her lover undefined –
Of both what was and what might.

Of her all she must give;
Her surrender complete,
Even her will to live
And her chance to compete.

For without the evening
Showing her underside
As food for the feeding,
Could the night be alive?

Every heart knows it must
Search for that which it seeks;
The trouble is for most,
A want unnamed it speaks.

Poem No. 21

The will to live
and the will to express
are the same to me.

Poem No. 22

And so the evening slips into night
with no marking this one from another,
but tantalizing the chance of insight
from a world I've yet to discover.
Here, where dark places are but places dark,
for your fellow man you need waste no fears
of horror to perceive the place most stark
which works nocturnally twixt your two ears.

Poem No. 23

And so the night creeps up on April's spring
Luscious it grows in its own vitality
Sinks under the weight of its newness.

Nightness descends on April's newborn green
The songs of the evening quiet to murmurs
A rowdy stillness defines the scene.

And so the evening slips into the night
With no marking this one from another
But tantalizing a chance of insight
Of a world yet to be discovered
Here where dark places are but places dark
For your fellow men – you need waste no fears –
With horror to preserve the place most stark
Works nocturnally between your two ears.

And so the night creeps up on April's spring,
Nightness descends on April's new born green,
Luscious it grows in its own vitality,
The songs of the evening quiet to murmurs,
Sinks under the weight of its newness,
A rowdy stillness defines the scene.

Poem No. 24

The crows' breakfast
Was a spectacular affair.
Eight hundred feathers,
And not a beak to spare.
Ripping plastic,
And a flurry of proboscis-poked holes
Launched this feathered feast
Which every sleeping heart knows.

So the night is split
By a wedge of sun
And the noisy morning
Of a noisy night
Has begun.

The crows' breakfast,
Was a spectacular affair.
Each one vying
For what little was there.

Poem No. 25

In lovely sorrow I find myself again
Asking what should I have done
His eyes were kind, but what would
He have me do for the kindness given
Is it the brand of stuff I look for
In every pair of passing doors
Would he be horrified at the question asked
Is it the brand of stuff he looks for
The answer could be so simple
Just a present of passing talk
Or a kind of thanks from, one so kind
But for the rest of sleep
I will wonder if that were all
So in lovely sorrow I find myself again
What should I have given him
The passing kindness of passing talk
Is it enough, even asking was it all?
Did I miss the mirror of my own heart
The kindest want I did not return
Was it the brand that we both look for?

Be it the look of my dreams?
I will ever be haunted thus.

Poem No. 26

May I tender a compliment
    to Lee of Melbourne;
        a bartender
        and a gentleman
        who sees a lot
    but says a little.
From me, no small praise, indeed.

Poem No. 27

That which can express
the inexpressible longing
shall live as long as man shall long

Cursed are they from the rest
who, for a measure are trying,
the length of their desire's song

For to long inexpressibly
is better than not to try,
though the measure of desire falls short

Poem No. 28 [3]

Moosh Pan, Moosh Pan,
you wonderful thing,
the qualities you demand,
drive bakers mad with skill,
and poetasters fat with glee.

Poem No. 29

To those who can tell
the length of their desire
in more than increments of sighs,
to them will living be beyond
scheming life's conspire.

Poem No. 30

Live while you can,
For Time's only plan
Fertilizers demand.

Poem No. 31

In lovely sorrow I sink again,
to the depths of a familiar deep,
while around my ears, the wells reveal then
new-sprung sources of emotions that creep.
Watch them gather, the white-shirted boys,
using notions of the usual kind,
words to hearten what hope destroys;
courage to replace that left behind.

Poem No. 32

God save me from the love
    I could feel for that face
From the reckless longing
    of his never-coming embrace

Why have the stars above
    deemed a torment for me
In my heart alone feeling
    the heartlessness of his glance

For the benefit of those lips
    a thousand thoughts could pour
Enough for the world's admire
    but enough for yours?

God save me from the love,
    for so easily could
I play your lovesick fool;
    could I escape my age
        In a love made for you.

Poem No. 33

    Youth has its own beauty,
        be it lovely or not.

Poem No. 34

The Moon's face is full
but it looks on my empty heart.
Endless shades of sun descend
to light a lightless form.

Poem No. 35

And, lo! Heaven and earth shall tremble
        and one become
When the wayward wants of Man
        manage a way.

Poem No. 36

three studies

Is my heart's affection my mind's desire,
        reduced all to the want, and want of the all?

The passion of Youth is in its inability –
        The longing of Age is for belief again.

Which be the measure of all,
        Love or Death? –
Which has power without the other.

Poem No. 37

Haiku:

Ocean grinds to sand
what river ground ever round,
where source meets its source.

Poem No. 38

*. . . from Kyushu
to an eighteen-year-old . . .*

Prelude:

Let me plow
the furrows of your brow
and then let me reap
their lovely sad burrows
for myself

Poem:

A butterfly's tongue
at length, it made you smile
and every inch of your face came aglow
with the wonder, at the delight
that I could find from
a butterfly's tongue

I wanted you so much;
to take you there
where the corners of your eyes
met smile and wonder,
the wrinkle of delighted brow;
God save me how I wanted you then
And how I want you now.
my love any better than these sighs?

Poem No. 39

prose fragment

Ben was Nathan's first love. He couldn't stand by without him
wanting, without needing for them to be standing as one; his
arms enwrapping Ben's slender waist, lips unable to breeze
over the folds of his deliciously soft neck. Nathan could not
stand alone ever again. Whether in person or in thought,
Benjamin stood within him.

Poem No. 40

To have a whole heart,
    to keep it ever at command –
Is it a want too large
    to cross over in a single span?

Poem No. 41

. . . a prayer . . .

Beauty make a place for me
where 'try' and 'lie' upsets raid –
where I, for the power of its form,
ever touch the mellow tenderness
granting my sorrow a chance to fade.

Poem No. 42

In confused splendor they stood,
two cans from twice
the other half of the world come,
but found no reception there even here,
in the hearts of enemies.

In confused splendor they stood,
two from twice the other half
of the world, my rejected homage
of the heart's intent.

Poem No. 43

Haiku:
俳句：

After days of rain
布団を出た *futon wo deta*
the welkin sky is welcomed
長雨の後 *naga-ame no ato*
by flights of futons.
空飛翔 *sora hishoh*

Poem No. 44

In a box I'll sit
With a rock on my head,
But no matter what the size
That box cannot hold my worth –
For that, dear reader, is in your eyes.

Poem No. 45

Winter seeps around me –
Finds me in my every pore –
Icy fingers and icy tongues
Slip in ears and between toes
With the flames of her passion.

Poem No. 46

A Jakarta Christmas

> *" . . . and the trees did blink for all*
> *in tropic shades of jitters,*
> *while garlands tacked to the wall*
> *the worst of the holidays embitters . . . "*

If all the world did want of me
something for it to say,
and write to it a story
of this unflinching day,
then I'd tell how the line of midnight
met the club still blinking away,
and a girl in lap was right
one moment slips the pay
to the nature of the night.

And Christmas is endured.

~

Part II:
Sweetest Grief to Hold
poems for Jimmy

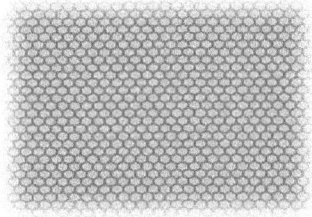

もし愛の言葉を書いたら
彼の意味に陥りますかあなた?
彼らの善意を愛撫して。。。

Poem No. 1 [5]

If I wrote some words of love to you
    Would you fall into their open meaning?
        Caress them for their good intentions . . . .

        That undiscovered concord of chaos,
        The guilt, hidden harmony of life,
        Beating away a measured metre lost,
        Seems the cause of all our disjunctions' strife.

        But, what if I said how much I love you,
        Pulling up a thousand sweet-rooted words,
        Each the more tender with love of you –
        Could you lose yourself to the touch of them?

If I wrote some words of love for you
    Would you then in my love recline?
        Allow me to dream myself alive . . . .

Poem No. 2 [6]

Poem:

In lovely sorrow I sink again
To the depths of a familiar deep,
Like fingers in aging gloves descend
To borrow themselves a state complete.
Around my descent, the white shirts land,
In lines as pure as bleach can render,
While I ask if any understand
The soundless graft of what I tender.
Here where I stand is murky and loud,
With some other's laughter swirling
As the ever-demand of that crowd,
Who seek division in a pairing.
   For who plummets to this depth of mind,
   Sorrow save him from the joy he'll find.

Postlude:

Ah, to have heart and voice the same,
Skill enough to bleed talent un-lame.

Poem No. 3

I want to love you more
   than jealous Time
   breath will allow

Poem No. 4

We all love
what we lack

and for the now
I lack a lot.

Among them, gold and such
and the eyes of esteem
to flow words onto me.

Yet, my pauperhood is made
of only one insufficiency;
of but one deficit.

For we all love
that which we lack,
and I but lack your love.

Poem No. 5

If upon me one line is writ,
Let it be that I loved you well.

Poem No. 6

Adrift sweet thoughts of you,
I set myself to this —
to dream some part of you
nearer me than this.

With all the will to potion,
of staining ink and sighs,
this paper's the emotion
of the sweet draw of your eyes.

So if you this knew,
what could you to me tell
to cast, and help me do
this grand sort of spell.

What music braced and steeled
might yet come from me to move,
that with a whisper you'll yield
to my dreaming dream of love . . .

Poem No. 7

What will they think,
The ones in whose eyes this will be –
From the first seers' blink
Till long after the end of me.

How long will they wonder
About the nature of this drive
To push paper with inpainted ink's blunder,
And this love an eternity to strive.

But they won't be linked
With we a privileged few,
Who celebrate Nature's instinct
To sentence us a life with you.

But if they who'll wonder then
Could see what I see now,
They would never ask again
Why through dulcet words I plow.

Your eyes would show them
Far better than I can do –
One glance would drive them
To desperate pen and paper too.

Poem No. 8

Sonnet:

If I could do this as well as I might —
Bring, say, a pine-clad Rocky Mountain peak
To loom over green valleys in its sight —
Spread for your account, wonders none-too meek,
What would you do if you knew their treasure
As well as that of your own mind glowing,
The greater value of sums to measure
By wanton reason of logic's showing?
If from mountain's height down to ocean's shore
Elements of earth and water conspire
To lend witness to my words heretofore
And let me borrow their great attire —
   Would then all the beauty seen in your eyes
   Prove my love any better than these sighs?

Poem No. 9

If I said I loved you
   and could say it well enough
      to raise from it the whole of a human soul . . .

What would you say of me?

Poem No. 10
A fragment

Sonnet:

The messenger of the morning,
Ascends the sky of the wayward night
With whispers of a coming sight
Greater than the sum of cold stars finding
Their numbers glory in cycles' height.

    I look at him in awe, (...)
    For all the all he means,
    That I envy in every line
    The eternal sun he brings.

Poem No. 11
Messenger of the Morning

The messenger of the morning
ascends the sky of wayward night
with whispers of a coming sight
greater than the sum of cold stars finding
their numberless glory in cycles' height.

    I look at him in awe,
    for all the all he means;
    here envy in every line
    the sun hard upon his back,
    pushing him to ever seek anew
    the darkness that he dooms.

The circles grow no more with addition,
and I no greater for the attempt,
for when all is sighed and written,
what more to me will be given
than where the herald of the morn was sent.

    Let me speak to you a fortune –
    the hags of Fate can tooth it out –
    in syllables of more than breath.
    Believe me, for all I can know,
    is where the ends will come to meet,
    new beginnings have chance to form.

So when accounts receive their call,
And if my love were meant for man,
Time becomes equal to the span
Of every 'I' I have signed in recall
Concerning how your eyes this love began.

    Messenger of the morn,
    rise up behind my love
    and whisper in that ear
    of these things I've said.

Though these rambles lack an order,
and in form are expression unserved,
tell him they lack not my own heart.

    Messenger of the morning
    wake up my love
    and deliver to his ear
    this rising dream of love.

Poem No. 12 [7]

With Bach in one ear
    and Roppongi in the other
    let me say my words of love.

And from the two worlds
    we'll one create
    if my words you can return.

Poem No. 13

The gold would corrode around my finger,
and music of the age get forsaken,
both rivers pause in possible linger
if the worth of love were ever proven.

But as I am, with eyes unseeing,
with a head unshown to connect,
have no fear of abjuring
bright thoughts with poor words that reflect.

About this advice I give to you,
though now stumbling and lame,
take care with what your heart you do
for this wordless want now knows your name

And I pray the gold to rust
in torrents down my longing;
an improbability crushed to dust
to prove your love bright and staining.

Poem No. 14 [8]

Love in the sky, with eye unblinking,
Watches from her scaffolding-height
My journey to a dawn,
And sends her jealousy to my place
To make company to what I must.

Through the night
as a child might run
from the gawks of eyes unkind,
I am haunted by this
and a fear of what could be;
a truth too grand to take.

Love has a price
costlier than should be,
the price of finding a thing
cheaper than the wealth of debt
can set a sleepy person free
if the cost of its seeming be.

Winter seeps around me
finds me in my every pore,
lacy fingers with icy tongues
slip in ears and between toes
spreading the springs of actions
in her own heat of firebrand.

So the winter night I must
with love above and ground below,
both unknowing care of what I trust
to find in another and there bestow
a light of my own sweet hope
rising higher than her unyielding scope.

To work so hard
at something too easy
to keep a fear as segregation
from what is a possibility
when chance keeps one too
as a division from you.

But now the resolve is made
and reason can keep her thorn
in the crown of cruelty,
no longer can it matter
to someone the likes of me
so long the jape of her royalty.

Through the night
one step is met by another
in purposes unkindred
by many a contempt
whose cause might be
to keep a mistake from me.

But unmoved by wind and sighs
the cause of this
is measured in increments
different of motives found
by words too often discovered
in the wanting of pity from that eye.

I run to the hope I have
that this chance I've taken
will be proven to a stave
a greater music not forsaken,
if fresh strength comes to me
to speak this love pf mine.

The image of a future yet to be
fills the space where steps cannot,
and brings a peace to seek
with half of me in conspiracy
'gainst rationale and morning's madness
as she wakes a fury in the dark.

Discipline lacks a mind untraversed
by the ridicule of facts
yet my heart holds your eyes
as rock-solid compass
to my navigator's task
and that to you I must.

And lo, my trip grows old
as around a corner I turn
to find an object of your desire
like symbol of that power;
and every drop black
both you and it control.

How wonderful to find it there,
how alive to feel it in my hands
and in my mind relive
the memory of its ride;
the black becoming me
and you between my legs.

Love in the sky, with eye unblinking,
Watches from her scaffolding-height
My brain and heart so dreaming
That love to me yet might be right;
And more than a mem'ry might this night free,
For if you knew of my love, might you in love be?

Sonnet:

If a passion can't find a form fit to touch,
Amid ever-shifting flows not to be moved,
Then why to all must be barred cunning luck such
As even a painter's skill has never proved?
When I saw you last, the sun made love to you,
A light hue unseen by human eyes before
Caressed like only imagination might do
When on the brightest form, more brightness might pour.
So, what is here drawn for you cannot say it;
All the power feeble in pen I contend
Cannot with the fresh force of me outlay it,
But as that light held you, so do I intend.
   When sun shall next behold your face, take warning;
   His touch might not be alone this fair morning.

Poem No. 15

How shall you be
when other loves
have made a home of me

Of all the will never-be's
yours will always stay
the sweetest one to me
if love has value to say

Poem No. 16

What shall happen in the years to come
when other loves have found a home in me
and surprise, your face again to me can become
a torment freed forward to look at me.
From all the never-be's, you will always stay
the song I never sung, the dream I only dreamt,
the sweetest one to me, the one I longed to say,
but on the truth I hung, and all the hope and cobwebs went.
What good the courage to tell you of my love
when you couldn't love as I hoped you could,
then finding the fool in me, looking like the words above,
I struggled with I began as best I could.
But when the future holds your face to me
A kinder torture I shall never see.

Love beyond the power to hold

                    Beyond every pain of me

Forever wants and wants again

                    I'll want you as long as I can

But of misery I have told

                    To kiss the fingers that

In love and love again

                    Bring you to me

How shall your face then be met

                    Torment and the sweetest

Through changing memories when it comes

                    Grief to hold

Like a checking vision sent

                    The loveliest unrequited

From this time, to there to-come

I'll kiss each finger and

Will the future make the better of me

Think them the best

With all the loves I could not hold

Since you I could not.

Will they all the better see

When they hold

The meaning of what love has told

Your face to me,

For when it comes to there

If love has warmed to me,

Against you

Then precession we will seem

They must be weighed

To the very act of love.

For if pain needs compare

Beyond the power to hold

None will match what

I'll want and want again.

What your love has to say.

Poem No. 17
Several years later . . .

I found an old poem,
A sonnet I had sketched,
And restudied it again,
And it was strange to see
That *messenger of the morn,*
That had caused me so much pain,
Was able to open a fresh wound –
What love had been,
It was again.

~

After Days of Rain
and other poems

Endnotes

Endnotes:

[1] "Poems written from my twenty-third year" The poems are presented sequentially from the calendar year in which I turned twenty-three years old. That means several of the early ones (up to No. 10) were written before my birthday in February, and thus when I was still twenty-two.

[2] "The war began on the evening news" makes reference to George John Mitchell, Senate Majority Leader 1989-1995

[3] "Moosh Pan, Moosh, Pan" is a phonetic rendering of *mushi-pan*, or Japanese steamed cupcakes. As snack cakes, they are usually sweet; in Chinese restaurants, they're usually neutral or savory. There was a commercial brand of cheese moosh pan that I was particularly fond of. See here:

http://www.heroine-love.com/japanese_mushipan.html

http://4.bp.blogspot.com/_44QpnGqjPEQ/Sp3 7MDRIHkI/AAAAAAAABDU/KEyyanDliZM/w1 200-h630-p-k-no-nu/P1010175.jpg

[4] "Sweetest Grief to Hold" is a collected section of love poetry written for a Japanese guy only a couple years younger than I, and whom everyone knew as Jimmy. I met him while he was bartending at a 'gaijin bar' – which means a weekday watering hole and weekend disco catering to local and international residents. This club, named *De-Ja-Vu,* was in the Kichijohji section of Tokyo, where I lived. We became friends, and although straight, I came out to him. A mutual friend of ours had already revealed my feelings for him, which seemed to only make us closer.

Wonderful person, he became the muse for my debut novel, and was the model for the fictional Dean in the book. *The Round People* may be found here in its entirety:

https://gayauthors.org/story/ac-benus/theroundpeople-anovel/

The epigraph appearing on page 47 is a Japanese translation of the opening stanza to poem No. 1: "If I wrote some words of love to you / Would you fall into their open meaning? / Caress them for their good intentions..."

[5] " . . . to dream myself alive" makes poetic reference to Oliver Wendell Holmes' *An Evening Thought.*

Oh, when love's first, sweet stolen kiss
    Burned on my boyish brow,
    Was that young forehead worn as this?
    Was that flushed cheek as now?
    Were that wild pulse and throbbing heart
    Like these, which vainly strive,
    In thankless strains of soulless art
    To dream themselves alive?

http://www.public-domain-poetry.com/oliver-wendell-holmes/an-evening-thought-written-at-sea-20202

[6] The "white shirts" refers to guys arriving in white shirts at the disco. They'd glow eerily under the strobing blacklights and colored spotlights while they danced with the girls they brought.

This whole poem is about being at the club, amongst those I didn't care very much for, wishing I was instead alone someplace with Jimmy.

[7] "Bach in one ear . . . Roppongi in the other." This is because Jimmy sometimes worked at the bar-owner's other club in the Roppongi neighborhood of Tokyo. Jimmy would call me during his breaks, just so say hey (and make me feel special), and the night the poem was written I was listening to Bach's mass in b-minor (which I'd just bought that day).

[8] "Love in the sky, with eye unblinking" For a longer elaboration on the motorcycle ride this poem memorializes, see the chapter titled *2 am* from my novel *The Round People*. The love in the sky here is a reference to the planet Venus active in the early morning sky; she is its messenger too.

https://www.gayauthors.org/story/ac-benus/theroundpeople-anovel/6